Original title:
Whispering Walls

Copyright © 2025 Creative Arts Management OÜ
All rights reserved.

Author: Clara Whitfield
ISBN HARDBACK: 978-1-80581-827-4
ISBN PAPERBACK: 978-1-80581-354-5
ISBN EBOOK: 978-1-80581-827-4

Reverberations in Stillness

In the quiet corners where echoes play,
Laughter bounces in a silly ballet.
Walls listen closely, secrets they share,
Tickles of sound dance high in the air.

When a chicken clucks in its own little way,
The floorboards gossip, not a word to betray.
Knocking knees cause chuckles, thuds and squeals,
The stillness chuckles; it cannot conceal.

Testimonials of the Silent Structure

The roof might creak like a grumpy old man,
While windows giggle, all part of the plan.
Every pebble whispers, 'I've seen it all!'
From toddler stumbles to grown-ups that fall.

A light flickers like it's had too much fun,
While shadows leap like a soft, playful run.
'We're here to witness,' the ceiling will smirk,
As the dog tries to bark and the cat goes berserk.

The Soft Call of Distant Memories

In the attic, a trunk holds stories and dreams,
Dust motes spin tales like magical beams.
Old toys join in with a nostalgic cheer,
As giggles and whispers come floating near.

Each crack in the plaster holds laughter unknown,
Recalling the antics from shivers to groans.
A chair softly rocks, with a chuckle it sighs,
At skinned knees and tree-climbs under bright skies.

Softly Spoken Reflections

Mirrors chuckle at the faces they've caught,
Each wink and grimace, a comic jackpot.
The clock ticks softly with a snicker and glee,
As every tick-tock calls out, 'Come see me!'

The floors murmur tales of lovesick retreats,
While curtains sway gently to the rhythm of beats.
Even the paint seems to giggle in hues,
As colors collide in hilarious views.

Beneath the Gale of Memories

The fridge hums softly at night,
Old photos skate out of sight,
Dancing shadows on the wall,
Pizza boxes hear it all.

Underneath an echo's sway,
I swear I heard my socks betray,
Last Thanksgiving's turkey rant,
Did it say, 'I'll haunt your plant?'

The Soundtrack of Solitude

The toaster pops a tune at dawn,
Each crumb a singer, wearing brawn,
Coffee mugs chime in delight,
A symphony at morning's height.

With my cat as a guest star,
She yawns and dreams of lands afar,
While curtains sway a waltz so grand,
In our duet, a rock band!

Secrets in the Grain

Wooden floorboards creak and sigh,
They gossip 'bout the days gone by,
Berets and mustaches tell a tale,
Of parties and spills and minor fail.

The beams chuckle at each new scratch,
Where did we put that little match?
It rolled away with laughter's roar,
To start a fire on the dance floor!

Echoes Bound by Time

The clock chimes loud to mock my fate,
It ticks and tocks, it won't be late,
Reminding me of socks gone missing,
In a universe of time dismissing.

The garden gnome, a wise old sage,
Assures me laughter's all the rage,
He's witnessed every garden plot,
And knows the weeds are always hot!

The Soft Sigh of Forgotten Rooms

In a room where dust resides,
Old socks and secrets love to hide.
Creaking floorboards laugh and tease,
While cobwebs dance in the gentle breeze.

A chair that rocks without a soul,
Claims to know the gossip whole.
With ghosts of laughter floating near,
Who knew this place could hold such cheer?

Curtains flapping like they're in a race,
Jazzing up the old, tired space.
They tell the tales of long-lost fun,
When the room was bright and the day was done.

Yet here we stand, with noses wrinkled,
The memories left, a little sprinkled.
In this echo of laughter's call,
We find the joy in the forgotten hall.

Timeless Conversations

Between the bricks, a chatter grows,
Where laughter lingers and mischief flows.
Pigeon meetings on the sill,
Debating crumbs with unmatched skill.

In every crack, a secret shared,
A wise old wall, a friend who cared.
With snickers hidden in the shade,
Witty replies cleverly laid.

The corners gather tales of yore,
Of socks that vanished, oh such lore!
As shadows bolt at every sound,
You've got to watch, they're all around.

These walls have seen a thousand jokes,
Whispered softly by invisible folks.
We giggle with glee as they unfold,
Old tales that never get too old.

The Language of Lichen

Upon the stone, the green stuff grows,
In silent laughter, it brightly shows.
It whispers puns in nature's tone,
A riot on the old gray stone.

With cheeky sprigs that twist and turn,
Tickling edges, they brightly burn.
In every crack, a punchline's twined,
Nature's jesters, unconfined.

They gather moss to tell their tales,
With silly shapes and funny fails.
In the damp, where humor swells,
They're the charm of forgotten spells.

So listen close to what they say,
In their odd language, join the play.
For in their laughter, bright and sly,
Lie secrets that never say goodbye.

Lingering Fables in the Walls

Each wall a witness to a jest,
From silly antics and weekend quests.
Echoes of giggles linger near,
As dust bunnies join in the cheer.

Hidden tales weave round and round,
In every nook, a story's found.
A chicken crossed the dusty line,
Becoming legend through time's design.

The plaster smirks at the old fun,
Chortling softly, it's never done.
For every knock and every thud,
Adds to the tales, a great big flood.

So grab a seat and lend an ear,
To nonsense best shared with a cheer.
For in these tales, the walls recite,
Laughter's twist in the fading light.

Unspoken Memories

In a house where laughter hides,
The fridge hums sweet, old jokes.
Dust bunnies dance in corners wide,
Where shadows tease and poke.

Squeaky floors share tales of clums,
Of trips and spills that time forgot.
A light flickers, and then it numbs,
As if it too has had a shot.

The cat meows of pizza nights,
Mouse tales that wiggle with glee.
As echoes of fun take dizzy flights,
In a realm of pure jubilee.

So gather 'round the ghostly cheer,
Of chuckles clanging through the air.
Each creak a laugh that we still hear,
In this space where joy is rare.

Resonance of Forgotten Voices

In the attic, a banter brews,
With cobwebs stretched like silly strings.
Old shoes tap dance and amuse,
While a calendar laughs at missed flings.

A mirror reflects a ghostly grin,
Of weddings, parties, and raucous laughs.
Photos cling to the dusty din,
Memories like awkward drafts.

In drawers, secrets lose their grace,
Like socks that wander on their own.
There's always one that skips its place,
A game of hide, the unknown.

As tick-tocks giggle on the wall,
Reminding us of all we lack,
These whispers bounce and twist, enthrall,
With every tick a comical crack.

Veiled Narratives

Behind the curtain, tales reside,
Of mishaps and a rogue shoe fly.
Hats on hooks hide secrets wide,
While squirrels conspire, oh my!

A tablecloth remembers spills,
Of juice and cake and wobbly chairs.
Where laughter curls and illness chills,
And grandma swears she's fixed her snares.

Timid mice skitter with glee,
Each squeak a punchline to behold.
As old clocks chuckle, set them free,
To tick-tock tales from days of old.

So flip the pages of this house,
And read the drafts of joy and fun.
In between the creaks, just espouse,
The sprightly tales yet to be spun.

Faint Footsteps on Dusty Floors

With every step, a tale unfolds,
A serenade of spryly shuffles.
Worn-out slippers and shoes of bold,
They hum along with tiny muffles.

In the kitchen, pots talk loud,
About the soup that spilled today.
Neighbors giggle, "Look at that crowd!"
As aprons wave from castaway.

As doors creak open, what a show,
A parade of mishaps and cheer.
Every stomp a silent hello,
Inviting laughter, scattering fear.

So tread lightly on these floors,
Where every echo leads a path.
To mischief hidden behind the doors,
And most certainly, a hearty laugh.

Sotto Voce in the Quiet

In a corner, secrets hide,
A talking lamp holds its pride.
The shelves giggle with their load,
Books sharing tales the world's bestowed.

A chair squeaks with glee, it seems,
Dancing to the sound of dreams.
Pictures laugh, their frames a-hoop,
At stories told in quiet troop.

The window yawns, the curtains cheer,
As dust bunnies pirouette near.
Echoes chuckle at the door,
Bantering as they keep score.

When night falls, the mischief starts,
Furniture plays its gentle parts.
With every creak, a jest is made,
In this cozy, lively charade.

The Gentle Caress of Dust

A dust mote twirls, a dance of grace,
Tickling the nose of the old lace.
Up high, a spider spins a joke,
On the shy mouse that might provoke.

Cobwebs hang like party streamers,
Hosting dreams and funny schemers.
The vacuum looms with a great big grin,
But dust just laughs; it won't give in.

Peeking from behind the clock,
Time itself is quite a mock.
With every tick, a stifled snicker,
As the old clock hands begin to flicker.

Even the shadows play their part,
As they bounce around, a playful art.
In this place, not a frown or gust,
Just laughter wrapped in gentle dust.

Ghosts of the Unsaid

In corners linger tales unsaid,
Where laughter mingles with the dread.
A ghostly chuckle floats about,
As rumors swirl with playful doubt.

The wallpaper peels with a smirk,
Hiding giggles of the quirky work.
Each crack, a whisper of past blunder,
Making walls laugh, a soft thunder.

In the mirror, a wink reflected,
All the truths carefully neglected.
Beneath the floorboards, whispers play,
Of silly pranks and jokes of sway.

Their voices rise in joyful cheer,
In the silence that we hold dear.
And as we wander, bold and proud,
We hear the ghosts sing soft and loud.

Silent Witnesses of Time

The hallway chuckles, echoes twirl,
As time spins tales of every girl.
Each portrait wears a grin so wide,
Capturing mischief they can't hide.

An old clock chuckles with a tick,
Matching steps with each little trick.
Rugs seem to giggle under feet,
As laughter weaves through every beat.

The grand piano softly sighs,
Its keys await to spread the skies.
Notes dance lightly in rhythmic spree,
Making melodies full of glee.

So here we sit, in quiet fun,
While shadows bask in the sun.
With each moment, laughter we find,
In the stories left by time, entwined.

The Language of Lost Dreams

In corners where secrets play,
A ghost of a thought drifts away.
Each smile a wink, a laugh will blend,
Like socks that hide from a laundry's end.

These echoes dance like penguins prance,
They stumble on words, lost in their chance.
A napkin's doodle tells a tall tale,
Of fish on bicycles or cats that sail.

Hushed Testimonies of the Past

The walls chuckle at jokes long gone,
With every scratch, a laughter's dawn.
An old chair creaks, a friend of time,
It joins the chorus, beats of rhyme.

Ghosts of the past in a dance-off spree,
They twirl in socks and sip their tea.
A whispered secret, a muffled cheer,
As slippers shuffle, we draw near.

Stories Etched in Quietness

On edges where memories fade like mist,
A couch sighs tales that can't be missed.
With each gentle knock, a knuckle plays,
A symphony of yesterdays.

A picture grins, while shadows blink,
Of awkward poses, what do they think?
A tale in dust, dressed with glee,
Of rabbits arguing who's got the key.

The Sound of Hidden Footsteps

Tiptoeing laughs in a sneaky race,
As shoes play hopscotch, a thrilling chase.
In cupboards and closets, they sneer and peek,
Each shuffle a giggle, so sweet yet bleak.

The patter of paws on a wooden floor,
As mischief whispers behind the door.
With socks that slide like ice on a spree,
These walls hold secrets, come join the glee!

Murmurs of the Ancient Stones

Once I heard a rock sneeze loud,
My friend said, 'Cover it, don't be proud!'
Stones chuckled as the wind did play,
Their giggles echoed, 'It's a windy day!'

In the corner, a granite boulder grinned,
Telling tales where time has thinned.
Laughter grew from cracks so small,
Even the moss joined in the call!

Pebbles tossed in glee, what a sight!
'Race us!' they shouted, 'Let's take flight!'
I joined them with my silly gait,
As laughter bounced, oh what a fate!

Old bricks chimed in with snickers bright,
'Watch out for that pigeon, it's taking flight!'
Crumbling faces, they gleefully shared,
Memories funny, no one was scared!

Silent Confessions

In the shadows where cobwebs cling,
I found a secret, oh what a fling!
Bricks blush and say, 'That's not my fault!'
As laughter bursts like a sudden vault.

Mossy whispers giggle, soft and small,
'Last year's party? What a ball!'
Spent the night with a shadowy crew,
Murmurs of mischief, never too few.

Hidden tales in a dusty hall,
'Can you keep a secret?' asked the wall.
With a wink, it swayed, 'Well, maybe so,
Depends on the humor of the crow!'

Cracks find a way to share stories wise,
Of cat antics and silly flies.
In silent corners where echoes tease,
History tickles, eager to please!

Hushed Greetings of the Past

Beneath the beams, the rafters sigh,
'Is that a ghost? Oh my, oh my!'
But it's just a bat with a hat on tight,
Flapping about in mid of night.

Walls lined up with snoozy bricks,
All sharing sentiments, what a mix!
'What's your secret?' asked one with flair,
'Just don't mind the dust, it's all in the air!'

Muffled chuckles, a mischievous crew,
'Let's play a prank, just me and you!'
They proposed a joke on a passing fly,
Never saw it coming, oh me, oh my!

Patterns of laughter, not so grand,
Told by the stones, heavy and bland.
Yet in their humor, I found delight,
Old echoes dance in the dead of night!

Soft Spills of History

Ancient tales in pebbled streams,
'Wait, are those my forgotten dreams?'
Laughter flows like water deep,
Secrets spill, too funny to keep.

Poured from the cracks in the wall's face,
'We once had a party in this place!'
A chair wobbled, joined in with glee,
Don't ask me how, but it's quite free!

'Oh dear, another ghost is here!'
Whispered the walls with a hearty cheer.
'Fear not, for all they want is a snack,
Silly spirit prefers a little crack!'

So join the stones in their playful jest,
History giggles, never a rest.
With each hidden laugh, we find a way,
To lighten the heart of each passing day!

The Breath of Eons

In a house of ancient bricks,
Laughter echoes with strange kicks,
The ghosts play pranks, they toss and tease,
In every nook, a funny breeze.

The door creaks loud, it makes a scene,
With every step, a ghoulish gleam,
A bowl of fruit, it rolls away,
As if the walls just want to play.

The windows chuckle, dust flies out,
While shadows dance, they spill about,
A chair wiggles, what a sight,
Join in the fun, it feels so right!

So here's to laughter, old and new,
To walls that giggle and join our crew,
In every crack, a story swirls,
In this old house, the fun unfurls.

When Silence Speaks

In creaky corners, thoughts collide,
Where quiet giggles often hide,
The silence here, a jester's mask,
In every hush, a funny task!

What's that? A crack? A tiny shout?
A mouse with dreams of flying out!
Did that chair just nod its head?
Or was it just a laugh instead?

The shadows squint, they wink, they tease,
A laugh escapes with every breeze,
A whisper here, a chuckle there,
In this hushed place, humor's rare!

So tiptoe soft, let laughter range,
For quiet spots can feel so strange,
A wink, a nod, the giggles spark,
In whispers bright, we leave our mark.

The Song of Ruins

Among the bricks, old tunes arise,
In crumbling walls, a sweet surprise,
A banjo plays, a catfish sings,
The ruins dance on broken springs.

With each crack, a note escapes,
A chorus formed by wall-shaped tapes,
The rafters hum a merry tune,
As dust motes spin, they jig and swoon.

A rusty nail, a tap, a thud,
The walls all laugh, collected mud,
Old paintings grin, with eyes so wide,
As history's quirks we can't abide.

So let us jive with laughter loud,
In faded places, we're all proud,
For every stone knows how to play,
In ruin's heart, we find our way.

A Palette of Hidden Hues

In colors bright upon the wall,
Each brushstroke giggles, hear their call,
A cheeky red, a funky green,
Together they make quite the scene!

Yellows sparkle in sunny glee,
While blues dance wildly, oh what a spree,
A swirl of laughter, pinks take flight,
In art's embrace, we feel the light.

The paintbrush dips, it paints a grin,
Creating stories kept within,
With every shade, a chuckle blooms,
Our palette bursts in joyful rooms.

So wander here in color's song,
Join the canvases that dance along,
In splashes bright, the fun ensues,
In every corner lies hidden hues.

Echoes in the Silent Space

In the corner of my kitchen,
A toaster makes a crackling sound.
It whispers tales of burnt bread,
And I laugh at crumbs all around.

The fridge hums a merry tune,
Balloons of ketchup rise and float.
Eggs gossip lively with the milk,
And donuts dream of being remote.

Old chairs creak with every step,
Tickling laughter in the room.
A shoe squeaks a silly laugh,
As dust bunnies dance with a broom.

A clock winks and tells no time,
It's stuck on five past tea for two.
But it still giggles at my socks,
In patterns far too bright for blue.

Secrets Beneath the Surface

The cat plots while the fish bowls spin,
A slippery plot in every fin.
Secrets bubble up with glee,
Each meow a hint, each gurgle a key.

The sofa's got a tale to tell,
Of midnight snacks and trips to hell.
Princess cushions hide the snacks,
While cushions hold the laughter tracks.

Beneath the rug, there lives a sock,
A rogue that swears it holds the clock.
It trips on tales of dancing feet,
And squeaks with joy during the heat.

The curtains twitch like nosy aunts,
Who giggle at your secret chants.
In corners where the dust bunnies play,
Are mysteries of an everyday.

Murmurs of Timeworn Stone

The garden wall has seen it all,
From giggly kids to soccer balls.
It coughs and wheezes with its tales,
Of summer sun and winter gales.

Pebbles gossip in a pile,
Each one pretending to be 'in style.'
They chat about the shoes that tread,
And who slipped by without a spread.

The old oak creaks with silent thoughts,
Of hidden spots and fairy plots.
Birds perch, nodding as they sing,
Unaware of the murmurs they bring.

A hedgehog pauses, takes a look,
At letters wrapped in shady nook.
Nature chuckles as it spins,
The tales of life where laughter begins.

Shadows of Forgotten Voices

In the attic where spiders play,
Old toys whisper of yesterday.
They giggle in the dusky light,
  Contemplating a new flight.

The mirror doesn't show just faces,
It reflects the lost childhood places.
It cracks a smile, it's got the knack,
  Of recalling every silly act.

Humdrum chairs with creaky sighs,
  Tell old jokes to the passing flies.
They reminisce of all that's missed,
Of tea parties where no one kissed.

The phantom cat with velvet paws,
  Prowls quietly, without a cause.
He chuckles softly, keeping score,
  Of every secret kept before.

Eavesdrops of Time

In the corner of the room, secrets hide,
Chairs giggle as the stories collide.
Footsteps shuffle, dust bunnies leap,
Silence shouts while the old cat sleeps.

Naughty whispers from a rusty beam,
Tickle the rafters, tease the dream.
Lampshades chuckle at the jokes they've heard,
While the fridge hums a forgotten word.

The clock winks, tickling each hour,
As the tea kettle brews its own power.
Posters giggle, peeling like paint,
They know deeds of the odd and quaint.

Oh, the days that sunbeams sneak,
Candles flicker, and floorboards creak.
Memories mingle, silly and bright,
In this house, all is pure delight.

The Language of Crumbling Brick

A brick hiccups under rain's gentle pat,
Laughing at pigeons, they're too fat!
Chimneys argue about who's the best,
While the garden gnomes take a nap, no jest.

Mossy whispers tickle the vines,
Crumbling joy between the lines.
A squirrel scribbles tales on the path,
While shadows giggle with a sly laugh.

Old walls gossip over passing cars,
Sharing tales of moonlit bars.
Every crack has a punchline bright,
As daisies dance in the fading light.

Mirthful echoes in the midday sun,
Brick and mortar have so much fun.
A chorus of laughter, what a delight,
In this wondrous play of day and night.

Tattered Stories in the Air

Tails of laughter hang in the breeze,
Like old pajamas tossed with ease.
The curtains smirk with a playful sway,
Whispering tales of yesterday.

Windows wink at the rambunctious trees,
As if they're sharing secrets with ease.
Rusty hinges squeak a tune so sweet,
While the dust bunnies gather in fleet.

A comic book flutters, pages aglow,
Starring a hero with little to show.
Socks in the corner join in the fun,
While the ceiling fan spins like it's on the run.

Oh, the giggles trapped in the air,
Tickling noses, beyond compare.
Every breath a chuckle, a jest,
In the realm where whimsy is at its best.

Beneath Layers of Echo

Echoes of laughter dance on the wall,
As chairs swap tales of the grand ball.
Beneath the floorboards, mice plot and tease,
While the stereo hums favorite CDs.

Clocks prank minutes and skip an hour,
Tickling silence with newfound power.
Old photographs wink at the passersby,
While remnants of glitter in corners lie.

The attic's alive with whispers and sighs,
As shadows launch jokes right up to the skies.
Crickets compose a quirky ballet,
To the tune of the light fading away.

Oh, the echoes that chuckle and twirl,
Spin stories of every boy and girl.
In this kaleidoscope of time and place,
Laughter lingers, a warm embrace.

Harmonies of the Abandoned Dream

In halls where echoes laugh and play,
The shadows dance and sway all day.
Forgotten shoes still tap and glide,
While walls conspire with nothing inside.

A chair once there now wears a grin,
As dust bunnies start to spin.
Old paint peels off like bad jokes told,
In the cozy chill of memories bold.

Framed photos grin in dusty frames,
Each smile hiding silly names.
A giggle slips through a broken pane,
As if the walls share every stain.

So join the fun, don't be aloof,
In the laughter of the crooked roof.
Where dreams are silly, wild, and free,
The funniest ghosts are here with me.

The Muted Chatter of Empty Rooms

In corners where the silence snores,
Conversations hum from unseen shores.
A distant tick-tock sings a tune,
Of silly stories under the moon.

The curtains flap like they're in on a joke,
While flickering lights create a cloak.
A creaky floor sings with a sigh,
As if to say, 'Oh me, oh my!'

Stained glass windows nod and wink,
While whispers of laughter start to think.
Each empty chair feels rather spry,
Contemplating how to fly high.

The past meets present in a goofy way,
Where echoes joyfully come to play.
In hollow halls, sweet giggles dwell,
A laughter spell that bids farewell.

Silence Singing in Brick and Mortar

Brick by brick, the humor grows,
With playful shouts that no one knows.
A paint chip grins from the wall so bare,
As if to declare, 'A fine affair!'

The rafters whisper in a quirky tune,
Chasing the shadows around the room.
Each empty nook has a secret punchline,
Where even the walls can feel divine.

Old doors creak with tales untold,
Of love and laughter, and maybe gold.
The windows chuckle at clouds above,
While bricks resemble a comic glove.

So lean in close and take a seat,
Among the echoes, warm and sweet.
The silence sings with a cheeky heart,
In this abode, all mysteries start.

Veils of Memory in Stone

In stone and mortar, secrets hide,
With giggles bubbling deep inside.
Where every slab begins to tease,
And laughter dances on the breeze.

A window's frame slyly winks,
As dust collects on forgotten drinks.
Creaky stairs tell tales of yore,
While the rooftops hum a silly score.

Vines weave jokes that twist and twine,
As ghosts of laughter intertwine.
A playful breeze tugs at the eaves,
And tickles the old, rusted leaves.

So listen close with a playful ear,
The echoes tease; the fun is here.
In veils of memory, laughter grows,
Among the stones where joy still flows.

The Gentle Breath of History

In corners where the dust bunnies play,
The shadows giggle in a quirky ballet,
They swap tales of footwear and fashion,
As time trips over with comedic passion.

Old portraits chuckle, their secrets untold,
As they swap stories of frocks made of gold,
While chairs creak softly, with rhythm divine,
They dance to the tune of a long-lost wine.

Mismatched socks tumble from the attic so high,
Claiming their fame as they wave goodbye,
The clock winks knowingly, ticks a sly beat,
As laughter drifts softly through tattered sheet.

Though the past might be silly, it holds a great cheer,
With echoes of giggles, it's perfectly clear,
That even old walls can have stories to share,
When the breath of history fills up the air.

Tales Whispered by the Breeze

A gust of giggles that tickles the trees,
Carries with it the chatter of bees,
They plot a great prank on the slumbering night,
As stars wink and quiver in pure delight.

The grass performs tricks in the light of the moon,
While crickets sing tunes of a silly cartoon,
Each blade has a joke, a pun to propose,
As the wind snorts laughter and joyfully blows.

Squirrels gather round for a grand ol' jest,
Debating the best way to rob a nest,
They tiptoe on branches, with flair and finesse,
In pursuit of a giggle, they won't settle for less.

Through rustling leaves, the giggling flows,
Spin stories of trouble, how mischief arose,
In the quiet of twilight, where whimsy lives free,
Tales abound, tickled by the tickling spree.

Silent Sentinels of Memory

The old phone booth appears with a wink,
It's witnessed the secrets, more than you'd think,
With hilarious voices, it rings and it toots,
Of love notes gone wrong and mismatched old boots.

A fence full of splinters has tales in its grain,
Of dogs on the loose, causing delightful disdain,
The paint peels in laughter, the logs join the jest,
In the chorus of silence, it knows all the best.

A rusty old swing set rocks in delight,
Recalling the antics of kids in mid-flight,
It squeaks out a sentence, then giggles a chord,
Each creak is a chuckle rehearsed and adored.

Oh, the memories linger, like bees with a buzz,
As walls tell their stories, like it's all just a fuzz,
In full-bodied laughter, they laugh to the end,
The sentinels grin, secrets they'll never offend.

The Soft Chorus of Echoing Times

In the baritone hum of the house so keen,
Old windows giggle, they've seen quite a scene,
Chairs banter kindly with their stories so grand,
Of games played in vapors of a whimsical land.

The kitchen recalls every faint, funny blunder,
As pots and pans warble, they soften the thunder,
A spatula spills secrets of cakes gone awry,
While laughter erupts like a raspberry pie.

Stairs creak with glee at each step of the way,
Reciting the tales of the family fray,
Three-legged races and tripping on shoes,
They echo the joy, the laughter, the blues.

Even the cobwebs are dressed for the fun,
As they dance in the breezes of memories spun,
With every soft chorus of echoing times,
They weave in the giggles, in rhythm and rhymes.

Shadows Speaking Softly

In corners where mysteries dwell,
The shadows confide and tell.
They giggle and chuckle, oh what a sight,
As they play hide and seek in the night.

A broomstick swats at a wandering sprite,
An armchair insists it caught a fright.
They pass silly secrets from lamp to wall,
Even the dust bunnies are having a ball.

The clock ticks loudly, yet they ignore,
Prancing like children across the floor.
They engage in tales of yesteryear,
Making time stand still, or maybe disappear.

So if you find your house seems alive,
With a jolly spirit that helps you thrive,
Just listen closely and you might discover,
The laughter that echoes, like no other.

Intimate Tales Underfoot

Beneath the old floorboards, stories do creep,
About jellybeans lost and a cat's secret sleep.
Squeaky shoes share their latest trip,
While the carpet giggles, doing a flip.

The rug remembers the spills of juice,
As the tiles gossip about a wild moose.
A sock puppet plots a great escape,
In the dance of the dust, there's no room for tape.

Sneaky cracks in the wood chuckle and tease,
As the vacuum hums a melody with ease.
They celebrate dances of the past,
Moving with rhythm, oh what a blast!

So do take a moment and look down low,
For beneath the surface, there's more than you know.
A symphony of quirk beneath your feet,
Where laughs linger long, and the fun is sweet.

Whispers from the Molding

The crown moldings gather to share some good cheer,
Telling tales of mischief that happened last year.
A wobbly chair joins the party in place,
While the walls wink mischievously, full of grace.

They talk of the cat who once leapt too high,
And gave the old curtain a scare or a cry.
With every soft creak, they recount the day,
When a brave little mouse led the children astray.

Baseboards chuckle at paint that has peeled,
Mocking the forgetful who clearly concealed.
Beneath every layer of dust, there's a laugh,
As they plan a reunion for the old photograph.

So next time you walk 'neath the arches and beams,
Remember the giggles, the laughter, the dreams.
For in every nook, there's a fun little tale,
Of the shy little spirits that never grow stale.

The Sound of Time Standing Still

In the hush of the room, you can hear it bloom,
A tickle of laughter that fills up the gloom.
Where seconds hold hands and stretch like a toy,
Time takes a nap, oh what a joy!

The pendulum swings with a goofy little grin,
Saying, 'Let's take a break, let the fun begin!'
It dances with dust, a soft little sway,
As moments get tangled in a playful fray.

Chairs chatter softly, serenading the glow,
While the windows wink secrets they can't help but show.

They conspire with clocks to forget all the chores,
Inviting the sun to come out and explore.

So let time stand still in a giggle and sigh,
With the whimsy of moments just passing by.
Listen for laughter in the air so bright,
For when time is paused, everything feels right.

The Stillness of Secret Passages

In corridors where shadows play,
A tiny mouse holds court today,
He's got a joke for every wall,
And giggles echo through the hall.

Behind the old, creaky door,
The rumors fly, they never bore,
A ghost in socks, so soft and sly,
He sneaks around with a pie in the sky.

The paintings wink, their eyes alive,
With every step, they start to thrive,
They share their tales of yesteryears,
All mixed in laughter, mingled cheers.

So if you hear a chuckling sound,
Just know that joy has been around,
In quiet places, fun will bloom,
Among the echoes, there's always room.

Hallowed Ground of Whispered Thoughts

In sacred spots, mischief resides,
Where theories roam like joyful tides,
A butterfly with a silly grin,
Makes up stories of where it's been.

The old stone bench with mossy charm,
Houses secrets of an ancient farm,
A chicken once plotting a grand prank,
Turns out that it just wanted to tank.

Piled up books holding quips and quarks,
Put on a show, let's meet the larks,
Each nibble of wit brings forth delight,
As these thoughts take flight in the night.

So lean in close, lend an ear,
Laughter bubbles, you're in for cheer,
In hallowed grounds where jesters dream,
There's always fun beyond the beam.

Hidden Echoes in the Corners

Atop the shelf, a sock puppet speaks,
With tales so loud, they tickle the cheeks,
Dust bunnies laugh, they conspire a plan,
To take the broom on a wild, wild ride, man!

Each nook and cranny holds quirky charms,
Invisible friends greet you with arms,
They scramble and dance, it's quite the sight,
As giddy echoes fill up the night.

A calendar cat with a running joke,
Says every day is a day to poke,
With witty quips from 1903,
His humor ages just like fine brie.

So if you stumble upon the strange,
Don't be alarmed, it's just a range,
Of hidden echoes, so jumpy and spry,
Let's giggle together till we touch the sky.

The Soft Breath of Stone

The pillars chuckle, they hold their breath,
As squirrels debate the tale of death,
Who will win in the race to the top?
Furry legs flying, they never stop!

The cool, old marble whispers a tune,
Telling jokes to the lazy moon,
Each crack has a story, each dent a laugh,
As the stones craft a crafty autoharp.

Charming brambles dance with glee,
To the rhythm of the buzzing bee,
The sunlight beams down, chuckling bright,
Creating shadows that prance in the light.

So linger a while, take in the fun,
With these soft breaths, let joy be spun,
A playful breeze tickles the air,
In the silent spaces, where silliness dares.

Quietude in the Architecture

In rooms where echoes play a game,
The wallpaper giggles, never the same.
Chairs tell stories of tea and sass,
While rugs roll their eyes as I walk past.

A chandelier winks with a glimmering light,
Swaying to thoughts of a party at night.
Corners crack jokes about dust and gloom,
As shadows perform a silly costume.

Windows share secrets with the moon so bright,
Gossipy breezes dance with sheer delight.
Floors creak with laughter, oh what a sound,
In this house of giggles, joy knows no bounds.

Lamps hum melodies, soft and absurd,
While spiders spin tales, swift like a bird.
In the quiet, a chuckle escapes my lips,
With every tick-tock of my watch that skips.

Murmured Blessings of Yore

In dusty halls where shadows lurk,
Old photos giggle as they smirk.
The portraits argue, who wore it best,
While misplaced slippers take a restful rest.

A grandma clock, ticking with flair,
Glances at the wall with a mischievous stare.
It tells of days filled with cake and glee,
Who knew the past could be so silly?

A faded rug hopes to catch a break,
As chairs gossip over tea and cake.
The curtain sways to the rhythm of fun,
While mice whisper jokes when the day is done.

Dust bunnies leap like acrobats bold,
Performing for stories that never get old.
The timeless walls chuckle, soft-spoken and bright,
As generations gather to share in delight.

Timid Revelations

A door creaks open, amazed at its luck,
To find the old mirror now plays with muck.
Reflections of faces, smiling confused,
Laughing at hairstyles that got overused.

A corner lamp, shy but keen to chat,
Spills all the secrets of old Mr. Pat.
With humor it lights up the room with a grin,
As tales of his cat and the squirrel begin.

The floorboards squeak like they wish to sing,
Their musical antics, such a funny fling.
In this space, where spirits convene,
Even the dust has a whimsical sheen.

Curtains sway gently, in rhythm with mirth,
Comedians hiding, all low to the earth.
In every crack, laughter echoes anew,
The timid revealings aim to amuse you.

The Whimsy of Erosion

Once proud and tall, a wall starts to laugh,
Cracks and chips map out a silly path.
Each erosion, a tale of great plight,
The bricks giggle softly in the dim light.

A paint splotch winks as if to say,
"I was vibrant once, now I'm shy in gray!"
Mortar cracks smile, revealing their flaws,
Who knew that age could cause such applause?

Windows rustle; they try to peek,
At stories unfolding, so joyous, so meek.
Sills embody days of laughter and tears,
Whispering jests from bygone years.

As weeds dance high in a spirited jive,
Each little bloom feels so very alive.
In the sway of decay, hilarity springs,
In the whimsy of life, chaos also sings.

Tones of Time's Embrace

In the corners they ramble, those old folks of yore,
Sharing tales of the past, just behind every door.
They giggle and snicker, in a language divine,
Swapping secrets of socks and the price of cheap wine.

Cracks on the surface hold stories untold,
Of dust bunnies waltzing, both timid and bold.
They nudge one another, with whispers of cheer,
As old kitchen gadgets recount how they steer.

The wallpaper peels with a chuckle and sigh,
I swear I saw it wink, as I walked by.
A brief flash of humor in every old frame,
As if life's little mischiefs were all part of the game.

In the bathroom, I swear the toilet will groan,
As it listens to gossip, collecting its own.
With each little flush, it chuckles aloud,
A secretive laugh amidst the crowd.

Murmured Confessions of the Abode

The windows jive with stories of sun,
Of laundry gone wild and that race where we run.
They laugh as they rattle, our mishaps they show,
Did you see that light bulb? It just shouted, "Grow!"

The floorboards creak with glee as I tread,
Reminding of snacks that I secretly fed.
They keep it a secret, their giggles a tease,
As I search for crumbs that were left with such ease.

Each shelf holds a rumor, a time long before,
About dusting or not, and the cat by the door.
They bicker and banter through every great quake,
In a comical dance of the fun they create.

One corner hums softly a tune so bizarre,
It sings of old trinkets and left-open jars.
The house has its quirks, its laughter ingrained,
In this silly abode, joy always remained.

The Subtle Language of Old Bricks

In the silence, they chatter, like best friends aligned,
Every chip and each fissure, a laugh intertwined.
They whisper of coffee spills, each paint mark a jest,
As if history knows they are truly the best.

The mortar holds secrets like a grandpa's old tale,
Of dogs who once trotted, and cats who'd prevail.
They chuckle at echoes, a piano means fun,
As it tries to remember the tunes that we sung.

Behind them, the laughter of laughter takes root,
An echo of leaps from a well-loved old boot.
They nudge each facade, as new stories unfold,
In a house full of giggles, so comfy and bold.

Even the chimney's a joker, puffing out smoke,
With each little gust, it provokes a great joke.
The bricks may be tired, but they wink as they stay,
A playhouse of banter in a humorous way.

Unseen Echoes of the Heart

Every thump of a heartbeat feels caught in the frame,
As walls wiggle close, whispering names without shame.
They share in the victories, marriages too,
Like a game of charades where the punchline is you.

The ceilings roll laughter, a tickle from above,
As I trip on the rug that says, "Get a glove!"
Painted with laughter, it winks at my night,
In the glow of the moon, all my troubles take flight.

Each crack in the plaster has tales it can tell,
Of late-night debates and of moments that fell.
They cackle with glee, those clever old walls,
As the dance of our lives through their echoes enthralls.

Even a breeze has its chuckle in store,
As it meanders through windows, slipping under the door.

In this merry old house, every heartbeat and sigh,
Is a story of love, enveloped in the sky.

Remnants of Silent Conversations

In corners where secrets seem to dwell,
A cat's yawn echoes, oh so swell.
A creaky chair grins with each sigh,
And the old clock chuckles, time flies by.

Beneath the layers, stories collide,
A pizza slice waits, pizza pride.
The ghosts of laughter bounce off the beams,
While shadows dance, or so it seems.

Tiny whispers flutter like leaves,
The chandeliers giggle, oh how it deceives!
Dust motes twirl in a wobbly jig,
As tea cups gossip, "What's your gig?"

In fading paint, a brush of mirth,
A scrawl of joy from the wall's birth.
Their sighs and snickers lace through the air,
Bringing humor in this quiet lair.

Veins of Time

Time trickles down the tiled floor,
With remnants of laughter, can't ignore.
The stairs hiccup as I ascend,
Whispering tales that never end.

Bottles giggle in the cupboard's keep,
While teapots snicker, half asleep.
The floorboards creak in a silly tune,
And shadows play with the white-tipped moon.

Frames wobbly dance, askew and grinning,
With snapshots frozen, yet they're spinning.
Through cracks in wood, life's chuckles seep,
Leaving today's secrets in mischief deep.

In this moment of quiet jest,
Walls stand up for a laughter test.
As the door squeaks a quirky hello,
Time wraps us all in a joyful glow.

Stories Etched in Patina

Upon the surface, tales unfold,
In rust and dust, laughter bold.
Muffled giggles in the wallpaper,
As colors crack, they slip and caper.

Carvings speak in a childlike glee,
"No more boring, come play with me!"
The floor's got jokes, it whispers low,
While chairs get cheeky, just to show.

Frames force a grin, they can't resist,
As memories glide, twisted and kissed.
Amongst the relics, a smile takes flight,
In corners where shadows play with light.

Each hint of aging tells a joke,
A story lives, evoking a poke.
In patina's embrace, laughter's hue
Connects the past to the silly new.

The Quiet Lament of the Cavern

In an echoing cave, mushrooms laugh loud,
Stalactites giggle; they're so proud.
Drips of water monologue with flair,
While shadows leap, unaware of care.

A pebble rolls and chuckles in stride,
As bats throw parties, they can't hide.
The cool air tickles, makes me snort,
With whispers of mischief, a joyful sport.

The walls hum a tune of long-lost jokes,
While echoes prance like merry folks.
In the ballet of darkness, the laughter sways,
As lanterns twinkle in magical ways.

Each creak and croon is a playful bed,
For stories skittering just ahead.
In this silent lament, joy takes its chance,
To lead the night in a quirky dance.

Voices Carved in Silence

In a house where laughter hides,
Old jokes dance and play the tides.
Pictures grin with secrets bold,
Walls recall tales yet untold.

Echoes chase the cat and mouse,
Squeaky doors act like a spouse.
Each creak and crack has a punchline,
A haunted giggle in the pine.

The floorboards giggle as we tread,
Stories bubble up like bread.
Every corner, a cheeky jest,
These rooms must be the very best.

In every nook, a prank was played,
A note, a sock, a grand charade.
Who knew a wall could crack a smile?
Here, humor travels mile by mile.

The Intimacy of the Unseen

In shadows, whispers curl and creep,
Tiny secrets that walls keep.
Cracks in plaster pass the time,
Each one hiding a nursery rhyme.

Furniture seems to roll its eyes,
As old socks tell their own goodbyes.
Chairs that clatter, tables that sigh,
Turn mundane moments into high spry.

The wallpaper smirks, what a prank,
As it listens to stories frank.
Absurd tales in dusty frames,
Who knew ghosts played such silly games?

In the quiet, chuckles ring,
A well-timed joke makes silence sing.
Unseen friends in shadows weave,
Making mischief, joy we believe.

Shadows Breathing History

Shadows giggle like a spy,
Echoes dance and flutter by.
In the corners, folks still chat,
Mystery meets a silly hat.

A ghost tips a glass, who would know?
History winks with a merry glow.
Can you hear that prankster call?
Always present, yet never tall.

Tickling dust in beams of sun,
Reminds us all how life is fun.
In every rustle, there's a cheer,
As past and present draw quite near.

With every creak, an old friend's joke,
Revisiting as laughter stoked.
Every moment, a time machine,
Witty shadows, bright and keen.

The Soft Heart of Stone

In a castle where stones align,
Lively tales spin like fine wine.
Each chip and crack, a pun to share,
As jokes tumble through the air.

A rock's tough facade hides a grin,
Softened heart beats loud within.
In every corner, laughter flows,
As history tickles, off it goes.

The grandeur sings, yet laughs too loud,
Echoes fold into a crowd.
Chiseled masks wear cheeky glee,
In silence, they welcome mischievous spree.

So raise a glass to all who stand,
These stone-beat jesters, oh so grand.
In stillness lives a hearty tease,
Where every glance brings silly ease.

Echos of Lives Unlived

In corners where shadows do play,
Socks find their mates, or so they say.
The chairs gossip of guests long gone,
While the cat naps on the old lawn.

Dust bunnies dance in a merry line,
Mismatched dishes sip on the wine.
Forgotten jokes hang in the air,
While walls giggle without a care.

Photos stare with a knowing smirk,
Recalling the fun of a quirky quirk.
They beam with laughter, holding tight,
To stories spun in the fading light.

In laughter's echo, old tales reside,
Serenade of those who tried and tried.
For every dream that slipped away,
The walls chuckle, come what may.

The Untrusted Secret of Stillness

A clock ticks softly in lazy dread,
While the fridge hums tunes that dance in my head.
The cushions conspire with a laugh so sly,
And the remote rolls its eyes, oh my!

Under the table, crumbs form a pact,
Whispers of snacks in the silence act.
Spaghetti, it seems, had quite a fling,
With meatballs joining in the swing.

Old books chuckle as dust arrives,
Mumbling tales of forgotten lives.
The lamp flickers like it knows too much,
Of secrets trapped in a silly hush.

In this stillness, the robins convene,
Discussing the tales that have never been.
With a wink from the moon and a giggle from stars,
The quiet giggles hide laughter in jars.

Untold Narratives of the Void

In a space where socks hold their breath,
And soup can lids conspire with death,
The pantry whispers of snacks untouched,
While the cupboards giggle, oh so crunched.

The fridge holds secrets like old-time clowns,
Of party leftovers and forgotten frowns.
An ice cream tub with a story to tell,
Of midnight trips, oh, that went so well.

Not all tales are built for the light,
Some shadows prefer to take flight.
The vacuum hums with a cheeky tune,
As it chases crumbs to the light of the moon.

In the void where laughter shall play,
Nonsense tales of the end of the day.
For every whisper that slips and slides,
The vacuum snickers as matter divides.

Where Silence Keeps Company

In corners where dust bunnies unite,
The riddles of silence become a delight.
Each creak of the floorboards, a voiced surprise,
That keeps the corners blinking their eyes.

A fork on the table hums a soft tune,
While the napkin folds like an old cartoon.
The ceiling might sigh, but it knows the game,
Of soft secrets woven into its frame.

Each shadow spins tales of giggles past,
Reminded of moments that faded fast.
The chair plays dead, but its grin betrays,
An ancient wisdom amidst silly displays.

In company where silence can thrive,
There's laughter hidden, oh so alive.
For every still moment that seems to fall,
The walls keep secrets, and chuckle with all.

Murmured Dreams of Architects

In a house that lost its plan,
A toilet was made the guest's fan.
Pillars dance with glee, oh my!
While ceilings giggle, oh so high.

Doors creak jokes that never land,
As windows plot their sneaky stand.
To the roof, a cat takes flight,
Barking at stars in the night.

Hallways wear mismatched shoes,
Painting the world in funny hues.
Chairs slide past, they mock and tease,
Chasing dust with silly ease.

This castle surely must know,
The secret laughter we all flow.
Blueprints filled with whimsical schemes,
Laughing echoes of our dreams.

Soft Shout of Yesterday

Yesterday shouted, but so soft,
A cat in a corner, too proud to scoff.
A fridge that talks back, it hums a tune,
While socks commit crimes beneath the moon.

Chairs debate whose leg is best,
As coffee spills out in a frothy jest.
The toaster pops with a wink and grin,
Making breakfast feel like a sin.

Cobwebs weave tales of old,
Of the dog who danced in dapper gold.
Walls wear glasses, laughing at tiles,
The floor cracks jokes, stretching a mile.

Traces of laughter, hidden and bold,
Ghosts of the past in stories retold.
Yesterday's whispers, never quite clear,
But they tickle the ears and disappear.

Fragmented Echoes in the Hall

In the hall, echoes play tricks,
With a floor that steps and sneezes quick.
A chandelier sways to a silent beat,
While rugs hold secrets of old, soft feet.

Voices bounce off the curvy wall,
Like marbles rolling, having a ball.
A clock winks slowly, losing the race,
As shadows attempt to change their place.

A lamp flickers with a gossip's flair,
It knows who's sneaking up the stair.
Posters giggle, glued to the scene,
While mirrors smirk, oh what a dream!

Fragments of laughter, light-hearted fun,
In the hall's embrace, we all run.
Echoes remind, with a playful draw,
That life is a game we play with awe.

Between the Lines of Silence

Silence has notes that tickle the air,
A vacuum hums as it catches a hair.
Chalkboards might crumble from all the grins,
As laughter erupts from the walls' chins.

Between the lines, antics unfold,
As furniture tells tales, both timid and bold.
The couch retells a joke from last week,
While the cat rolls her eyes and squeaks.

Dishes collide like they've lost a bet,
Summoning echoes that no one forgets.
In this stillness, a ruckus is born,
With the bread loaf snickering, slightly worn.

So let's not fret in this quiet space,
Where joy in silence finds its place.
Between the lines, laughter waits,
In the cozy nooks, where fun creates.

Voices of the Ancients

In the attic, I hear a scare,
A ghostly giggle floats through the air.
They argue over who broke the vase,
While I just giggle, watching their chase.

The walls chuckle at their goofy fight,
With echoes of laughter, pure delight.
An old chair creaks as if to call,
"Who needs a ghost when you have a brawl?"

Dust bunnies dance, as shadows spin,
One steals a cookie, oh what a sin!
Another shouts, "Hand that back here!"
And silence falls, the walls must hear.

With every story steeped in jest,
The ancient tales are truly the best.
So listen close, it's all a thrill,
In these moments, time stands still.

The Soliloquy of the Structure

The beams above are wise and old,
With tales of laughter yet untold.
They creak and groan as if to say,
"Watch out for kids who love to play!"

A sneaky squirrel once took a nap,
On a roof beam, caught in a trap.
He rolled and tumbled, oh what a scene,
As walls chuckled, the floors turned green!

The windows gossip, a humorous crew,
Spying on neighbors, what will they do?
They laugh at the cat who chases his tail,
Wishing for snacks, they tell quite the tale.

Structured with joy, this house of mine,
Produces giggles like fine aged wine.
Each corner holds a secret grin,
And every crack lets the humor in.

The Secret Symphony of Stone

Stones in the garden hum a tune,
Under the watch of a laughing moon.
They tell tales of kids and their dreams,
As the breeze spills laughter in streams.

A gnome on the porch, begrudging his fate,
Says he lost a race to a snail named Kate.
The stones chuckle, their rhythm so sly,
While the flowers bloom and tell a lie.

The fence plays a note, the gate takes a bow,
The laughter echoes in every row.
As bees buzz in, they're part of the show,
Creating sweet music, delightful and low.

In this secret space, melodically bright,
The stones hold the secrets of endless delight.
With every heartbeat, they dance and prance,
Inviting us all to join in the dance.

Apparitions of the Past

When dusk falls low, the shadows peep,
Old friends arrive, they don't miss a beat.
They stumble around, each with a grin,
Telling tales of where they've been.

One claims they dated a broomstick tall,
Another insists on a dance off ball.
The walls shake lightly with giggles so loud,
As they recount pranks that made them so proud.

A cat appears, they all take a pause,
"Hey Tommy, knock it off with your claws!"
They roll their eyes, then laugh away,
What stories will emerge by light of day?

From dusty corners, they share their quirks,
Nostalgically woven like friendly works.
So let them chat, let the mischief commence,
In every echo, there's a hint of suspense.

www.ingramcontent.com/pod-product-compliance
Lightning Source LLC
Chambersburg PA
CBHW070323120526
44590CB00017B/2793